THE SONGS OF ANDREW LLOYD WEBBER™
40 OF HIS GREATEST HITS

Andrew Lloyd Webber™ is a trademark owned by Andrew Lloyd Webber.

ISBN 978-1-4768-1399-8

HAL•LEONARD®

7777 W. BLUEMOUND RD. P.O. BOX 13819 MILWAUKEE, WI 53213

In Australia Contact:
Hal Leonard Australia Pty. Ltd.
4 Lentara Court
Cheltenham, Victoria, 3192 Australia
Email: ausadmin@halleonard.com.au

Visit Hal Leonard Online at
www.halleonard.com

CONTENTS

ALL I ASK OF YOU

from THE PHANTOM OF THE OPERA

CLARINET

Music by ANDREW LLOYD WEBBER
Lyrics by CHARLES HART
Additional Lyrics by RICHARD STILGOE

ANOTHER SUITCASE IN ANOTHER HALL

from EVITA

Clarinet

Words by TIM RICE
Music by ANDREW LLOYD WEBBER

AMIGOS PARA SIEMPRE
(Friends for Life)
(The Official Theme of the Barcelona 1992 Games)

CLARINET

Music by ANDREW LLOYD WEBBER
Lyrics by DON BLACK

ANGEL OF MUSIC
from THE PHANTOM OF THE OPERA

CLARINET

Music by ANDREW LLOYD WEBBER
Lyrics by CHARLES HART
Additional Lyrics by RICHARD STILGOE

ANY DREAM WILL DO

from JOSEPH AND THE AMAZING TECHNICOLOR® DREAMCOAT

Clarinet

Music by ANDREW LLOYD WEBBER
Lyrics by TIM RICE

AS IF WE NEVER SAID GOODBYE

from SUNSET BOULEVARD

Clarinet

Music by ANDREW LLOYD WEBBER
Lyrics by DON BLACK and CHRISTOPHER HAMPTON,
with contributions by AMY POWERS

CLOSE EVERY DOOR

from JOSEPH AND THE AMAZING TECHNICOLOR® DREAMCOAT

Clarinet

Music by ANDREW LLOYD WEBBER
Lyrics by TIM RICE

DON'T CRY FOR ME ARGENTINA
from EVITA

Clarinet

Words by TIM RICE
Music by ANDREW LLOYD WEBBER

EVERYTHING'S ALRIGHT

from JESUS CHRIST SUPERSTAR

CLARINET

Words by TIM RICE
Music by ANDREW LLOYD WEBBER

I DON'T KNOW HOW TO LOVE HIM
from JESUS CHRIST SUPERSTAR

Clarinet

Words by TIM RICE
Music by ANDREW LLOYD WEBBER

HIGH FLYING, ADORED

from EVITA

CLARINET

Words by TIM RICE
Music by ANDREW LLOYD WEBBER

I AM THE STARLIGHT

from STARLIGHT EXPRESS

CLARINET

Music by ANDREW LLOYD WEBBER
Lyrics by RICHARD STILGOE

I BELIEVE MY HEART

from THE WOMAN IN WHITE

Clarinet

Music by ANDREW LLOYD WEBBER
Lyrics by DAVID ZIPPEL

I'M HOPELESS WHEN IT COMES TO YOU

from STEPHEN WARD

CLARINET

Music by ANDREW LLOYD WEBBER
Book and Lyrics by DON BLACK
and CHRISTOPHER HAMPTON

LEARN TO BE LONELY

from THE PHANTOM OF THE OPERA

Clarinet

Music by ANDREW LLOYD WEBBER
Lyrics by CHARLES HART

LIGHT AT THE END OF THE TUNNEL

from STARLIGHT EXPRESS

CLARINET

Music by ANDREW LLOYD WEBBER
Lyrics by RICHARD STILGOE

LOVE CHANGES EVERYTHING

from ASPECTS OF LOVE

CLARINET

Music by ANDREW LLOYD WEBBER
Lyrics by DON BLACK and CHARLES HART

MEMORY
from CATS

Clarinet

Music by ANDREW LLOYD WEBBER
Text by TREVOR NUNN after T.S. ELIOT

LOVE NEVER DIES

from LOVE NEVER DIES

CLARINET

Music by ANDREW LLOYD WEBBER
Lyrics by GLENN SLATER

MAKE UP MY HEART

from STARLIGHT EXPRESS

CLARINET

Music by ANDREW LLOYD WEBBER
Lyrics by RICHARD STILGOE

MR. MISTOFFELEES
from CATS

CLARINET

Music by ANDREW LLOYD WEBBER
Text by T.S. ELIOT

THE MUSIC OF THE NIGHT

from THE PHANTOM OF THE OPERA

Clarinet

Music by ANDREW LLOYD WEBBER
Lyrics by CHARLES HART
Additional Lyrics by RICHARD STILGOE

NO MATTER WHAT

from WHISTLE DOWN THE WIND

Clarinet

Music by ANDREW LLOYD WEBBER
Lyrics by JIM STEINMAN

Moderately slow

Slower

THE PERFECT YEAR
from SUNSET BOULEVARD

Clarinet

Music by ANDREW LLOYD WEBBER
Lyrics by DON BLACK
and CHRISTOPHER HAMPTON

THE PHANTOM OF THE OPERA
from THE PHANTOM OF THE OPERA

Clarinet

Music by ANDREW LLOYD WEBBER
Lyrics by CHARLES HART
Additional Lyrics by RICHARD STILGOE
and MIKE BATT

Moderately fast

PIE JESU
from REQUIEM

CLARINET

By ANDREW LLOYD WEBBER

STARLIGHT EXPRESS
from STARLIGHT EXPRESS

CLARINET

Music by ANDREW LLOYD WEBBER
Lyrics by RICHARD STILGOE

THE POINT OF NO RETURN
from THE PHANTOM OF THE OPERA

CLARINET

Music by ANDREW LLOYD WEBBER
Lyrics by CHARLES HART
Additional Lyrics by RICHARD STILGOE

41

SEEING IS BELIEVING

from ASPECTS OF LOVE

Clarinet

Music by ANDREW LLOYD WEBBER
Lyrics by DON BLACK and CHARLES HART

STICK IT TO THE MAN

from SCHOOL OF ROCK

CLARINET

Music by ANDREW LLOYD WEBBER
Lyrics by GLENN SLATER

Medium Blues Rock

SUPERSTAR
from JESUS CHRIST SUPERSTAR

CLARINET

Words by TIM RICE
Music by ANDREW LLOYD WEBBER

TELL ME ON A SUNDAY
from SONG & DANCE

Clarinet

Music by ANDREW LLOYD WEBBER
Lyrics by DON BLACK

TAKE THAT LOOK OFF YOUR FACE
from SONG & DANCE

CLARINET

Music by ANDREW LLOYD WEBBER
Lyrics by DON BLACK

THINK OF ME
from THE PHANTOM OF THE OPERA

Clarinet

Music by ANDREW LLOYD WEBBER
Lyrics by CHARLES HART
Additional Lyrics by RICHARD STILGOE

'TIL I HEAR YOU SING

from LOVE NEVER DIES

Clarinet

Music by ANDREW LLOYD WEBBER
Lyrics by GLENN SLATER

UNEXPECTED SONG
from SONG & DANCE

CLARINET

Music by ANDREW LLOYD WEBBER
Lyrics by DON BLACK

Gently

WHISTLE DOWN THE WIND

from WHISTLE DOWN THE WIND

CLARINET

Music by ANDREW LLOYD WEBBER
Lyrics by JIM STEINMAN

Moderately

WISHING YOU WERE SOMEHOW HERE AGAIN

from THE PHANTOM OF THE OPERA

CLARINET

Music by ANDREW LLOYD WEBBER
Lyrics by CHARLES HART
Additional Lyrics by RICHARD STILGOE

Moderately slow

WITH ONE LOOK

from SUNSET BOULEVARD

Clarinet

Music by ANDREW LLOYD WEBBER
Lyrics by DON BLACK and CHRISTOPHER HAMPTON,
with contributions by AMY POWERS

YOU MUST LOVE ME
from the Cinergi Motion Picture EVITA

Clarinet

Words by TIM RICE
Music by ANDREW LLOYD WEBBER